101
BOSSY COW
JOKES

Katy Hall & Lisa Eisenberg
illustrated by Don Orehek

SCHOLASTIC INC.
New York Toronto London Auckland Sydney

ISBN 0-590-42263-4

Copyright© 1989 by Katy Hall and Lisa Eisenberg. All rights reserved. Published by Scholastic Inc.

12 11 10 9 8   5 6 7 8 9/9 0/0

Printed in the U.S.A.   01

First Scholastic printing, June 1989

To the whole herd . . .
Leigh, Kate, Annie, and Thomas

COW ABOUT THAT?

What do you call a cow that's just had a baby?

De-calfinated!

What do you get from pampered cows?

Spoiled milk!

Why does a cow wear a bell?

Because her horn doesn't work!

What's another name for a
cowhand?

Hamburger helper!

What do cows do when they're
introduced?

They give each other a milk shake!

When was beef the highest?

When the cow jumped over the moon!

HOW AMOOSING!

What do cows read at the breakfast table?

The moospaper!

What do you get when you cross a cow with a kangaroo?

A kangamoo!

What famous painting do cows love to look at?

The Moona Lisa!

What do cows call Frank Sinatra?

Old Moo Eyes!

Farmer One: If you had a gun and you were being chased by a bull and a mountain lion, which one would you shoot first?
Farmer Two: The mountain lion. You can always shoot the bull!

STEER CLEAR OF THESE!

What do you call a sleeping steer?

A bull dozer!

What kind of bulls giggle?

Laughingstock!

How do bulls drive their cars?

They steer *them!*

Farmer Bill: Is there big money in the cattle business?
Farmer Will: So I've herd!

A summer visitor asked the farmer how long cows should be milked.

"Oh, I reckon about the same as short ones!" the farmer answered.

KNOCK, KNOCK!
MOO'S THERE?

Knock, knock!
Moo's there?
Pasture.
Pasture who?
Pasture bedtime, isn't it?

Knock, knock!
Moo's there?
Moscow.
Moscow who?
Moscow gives more milk than Pa's
    cow!

Knock, knock!
Moo's there?
Beef.
Beef who?
Beefore I tell you, let me in!

Knock, knock!
Moo's there?
Howie.
Howie who?
Howie getting away from that
    charging bull over there?

COW COWNTRY

In what state will you find the most cows?

Moo York!

Why don't the people in Sweden export cattle?

They like to keep their Stockholm!

What South American dance do cows like to do?

The Rump-a!

Ned: Your Honor, it was an accident! I had to run into the fence to keep from hitting the cow!

Judge: Was it a Jersey cow?

Ned: I don't know — I didn't see her license plate!

What do cows wear when they're
vacationing in Hawaii?

Moo moos!

Cowhand Sal: If a bull is chasing you, what steps should you take?
Cowhand Al: The longest ones I could!

What country do cows love to visit?

Moo Zealand!

CABULL TV GUIDE

9 A.M. Kaptain Kangarmoo
10 A.M. Beef-witched
11 A.M. Cowtoon Express
12 P.M. Let's Milk a Deal
1 P.M. Moosbreak
2 P.M. Leave It to Beefer
3 P.M. M*O*O*S*H
4 P.M. Fodder Knows Best
5 P.M. Moo Gyver
6 P.M. Bull Cowsby Show

UNMIS-STEAK-ABLY SILLY!

Where did the bull carry his stock-market report?

In his beef case!

What did the calf say to the silo?

"Is my fodder in there?"

How did the calf's final exam turn out?

Grade A!

Does running out of a burning barn make a cow unusual?

No, only medium rare!

Where do cows go on dates?

To the moovies!

Why did Bossy slug Roy Rogers?

She heard he was a cowpuncher!

COWTOON TIME!

Cowboy: I broke three wild bulls
  this morning.
City Slicker: How careless of you!

City Slicker: If you see a whole field of cows, what's a fast way to figure out how many cattle there are?

Farmer: Count the hooves and divide by four!

MOO HOO!

A moo hoo is a riddle with a rhyming answer.

What's a moo hoo for a young calf?

A new moo!

What's a moo hoo for a cattle dinner?

Cow chow!

What's a moo hoo for a cow barn on a holiday?

A merry dairy!

What's a moo hoo for a stuffed steer?

A full bull!

What's a moo hoo for a bull's haircut?

A steer shear!

What's a moo hoo for a bunch of weirdo cattle?

A nerd herd!

COW CROSSING

If you crossed two cows with a flock of ducks, what would you get?

Milk and quackers!

If you crossed a cow with a goat, what would you get?

Half and half!

If you crossed a cow with an insect, what would you get?

A moosquito!

If you crossed a cow with Michael Jackson, what song would you get?

"Beef It!"

GOING TO
THE MOOVIES!

**Favorite Cow Moovies
and Shows of All Time**

Close Encownters of the Curd Kind

The Sound of Moosic

The Godfodder

Young Frankensteer

Hoof Framed Roger Rabbit?

Stand by Moo

Cowrate Kid

Favorite Cowlebrities
of All Time

Flank Sinatra

Moodonna

Calfarine Hepbarn

Moolon Barndo

Bully Dee Williams

Liz Tailor

Shirley MilkLaine

YOUR BRAND
OF HUMOOR?

Where do steers go to dance?

To the Meat Ball!

Why don't cows ever have any
money?

Because the farmers milk them dry!

Where do Russian cows come from?

Moscow!

Where do Danish cows come from?

Cowpenhagen!

What magazine makes cows
stampede to the newsstand?

Cows-mopolitan!

What has four legs and goes, "Oom!
Oom!"?

A cow walking backwards!

MOORE COWTOONS!

Cow: Why don't you shoo those
  flies?
Bull: Aw, let 'em go barefoot!

MOORE
KNOCK, KNOCK!
MOO'S THERE?

Knock, knock!
Moo's there?
Butcher!
Butcher who?
Butcher hand on that milk pail
  before Bossy kicks it over!

Knock, knock!
Moo's there?
Button!
Button who?
Button in front of me for a glass of
  milk is rude!

Knock, knock!
Moo's there?
Dairy!
Dairy who?
Dairy go into that field with the
    raging bull?

Knock, knock!
Moo's there?
Moo!
Moo hoo?
Moove on to another kind of joke,
    please!

THE COWMEDY HOUR!

How did the cow feel when she couldn't give any milk?

Like an udder failure!

What do you call a bull that's sent overseas by boat?

Shipped beef!

How does a cow do math?

With a cowculator!

Why are cows made for dancing?

They're all born hoofers!

COW RIDDLES

What do you get from a forgetful cow?

Milk of amnesia!

What do you get from an invisible cow?

Evaporated milk!

What do you get from a cow with a split personality?

Half and half!

What do you get from a cow on the North Pole?

Cold cream!

Why do cows think cooks are mean?

They whip cream!

What kind of cow goes, "Beeeeep, beeeeep!"

A longhorn!

MOORE COWTOONS

Scientist: I've just discovered a method for making wool out of milk!

Reporter: But doesn't that make the cow feel a little sheepish?

Farmer 1: That bull you sold me is a lazy good-for-nothing!

Farmer 2: I *told* you he was a bum steer!

Clem: Pa's being chased by a bull!

Mr. Frumper: Well, what in tarnation do you want me to do about it?

Clem: Sell me some film for my camera!

MOORE MOO HOOS

What's a moo hoo for a tug-of-war
between two longhorns?

A bull pull!

What's a moo hoo for a baby cow's
giggle?

A calf laugh!

What's a moo hoo for grazing
school?

Grass class!

What's a moo hoo for a cow's cud?

A moo chew!

What's a moo hoo for the sound you hear when a cow spits?

A cud thud!

What's a moo hoo for a darling bull?

A dear steer!

THE BOOK MOOBILE

(Books that have sold cowntless cowpies!)

Mooby Dick

The Collected Works of William Shakesteer

Good Night Moooon

The Herdy Boys

Nancy Drew Moosteries

Pippi Longhornstocking

Little Cows on the Prairie

Moory Poppins

The Cownt of Moonte Cristo

The Three Mooosketeers

Autobiography of Benjamin Flanklin

HERD THIS ONE?

What do you call it when one bull spies on another bull?

A steak-out!

When a bull wants to listen to a cassette, what does he put on his head?

Steer phones!

What kind of cows do you find in Alaska?

Eski-moos!

SAL: Did you hear about the farmer who lost control of his tractor in the cow pasture?

AL: No! Did he hurt the cows?

SAL: No, he just grazed them!

A COWRES LINE
(of Bossy's favorite singers)

The Beefles

Barnbra Streisand

Natalie Cowl

Mel Tormoo

Lena Horn

Bing Cowsby

Bruce Springsteer

Pat Barnatar

Bully Joel

Moo-2

Aretha Flanklin

Eddie Moo-ney

MOORON JOKES

Why did the mooron give the sleepy cow a hammer?

He wanted her to hit the hay!

Why did the mooron give the bull a credit card?

He wanted to see him charge!

Where did the mooron take the baby cow to eat?

To the calf-ateria!

What did the mooron say when he saw the milk cartons in the grass?

"Hey! Look at the cow's nest!"

EVEN MOORE COWTOONS

City Slicker: What do you use this rope for?
Cowboy: I use it to catch cattle.
City Slicker: Oh really? What do you use for bait?

PRIME RIBS

Ned: Did you hear that Canada sold the U.S. a large herd of bison?

Ted: Oh. Did Canada send the U.S. a buffalo bill?

Lil: Did you know that I'm a dairy maid at a chocolate factory?

Jill: That's strange. What do you do?

Lil: I milk chocolates!

Jim: How did that bullfight come out?

Tim: Oh, it was a toss-up!

MOORE
KNOCK, KNOCK!
MOO'S THERE?

Knock, knock!
Moo's there?
Candy.
Candy who?
Candy cow jump over the moon?

Knock, knock!
Moo's there?
Carmen!
Carmen who?
Carmen get me out of the middle of
    this stampede!

Knock, knock!
Moo's there?
Dishes!
Dishes who?
Dishes the right side of the cow for
   milking!

Knock, knock!
Moo's there?
Elsie!
Elsie who?
Elsie you behind the barn after
   supper!

BULLY FOR THESE!

What do you get from a short-legged cow?

Dragon milk!

Why did the farmer feed money to his cow?

He wanted rich milk!

What would you hear at a cow concert?

Moo-sic!

Why is the barn always so noisy?

All the cows have horns!

JUNIOR COWLLEGE

Teacher: What do you call a group of cattle sent into orbit?

Student: The first herd shot round the world!

Teacher: Name five things that contain milk.
Student: Butter, cheese, ice cream . . . and two cows!

THAT'S INCUDIBULL!

If you make a cow angry, how will she get even?

She'll cream you!

What do you call a bull that runs into a threshing machine?

Hamburger!

What two members of the cow family go everywhere with you?

Your calves!

Why couldn't the cow leave the farm?

She was pasteurized!

Why was the calf so snobby?

He thought he was a cutlet above the rest!

Why wouldn't anyone play with the little longhorn?

He was too much of a bully!

CATTLE COUNTRY!

UNITED STATES
CATTLE

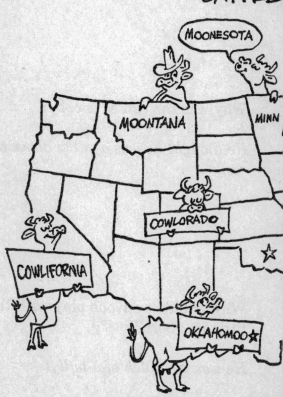

A city slicker climbed over a fence into a field to pick some flowers. Just then, he noticed a bull nearby.

City Slicker: Say, farmer. Is that bull safe?

Farmer: Well, he's a lot safer than you are right now!

Lem: What would you get if you crossed a cow with a rabbit?

Jem: Hare in your milk!

THE TAIL END OF THE MOO HOOS!

What is a moo hoo for a delightful ranch owner?

A charmer farmer!

What is a moo hoo for a cow fight?

A cattle battle!

What is a moo hoo for a sheepish steer?

A woolly bully!

What is a moo hoo for a cow that fell into the thresher?

Ground round!

What is a moo hoo for steak that came late?

Filet delay!

What is a moo hoo for the bucket that goes at the back end of the cow?

A tail pail!

TOP-SELLING MOOSICAL COWSETTES

Mooon River

I Herd It Through the Grapevine

Now I Know My A, Beef, C's

Go Tail It on the Mountain

Rope, Rope, Rope Your Boat

Twinkle, Twinkle Little Steer

I've Got You Udder My Skin

Oklahomoo

THE TAIL END OF KNOCK, KNOCK! MOO'S THERE?

Knock, knock!
Moo's there?
Emma.
Emma who?
Emma fraid to milk the cow!

Knock, knock!
Moo's there?
Heifer.
Heifer who?
Heifer cow is better than no cow!

Knock, knock!
Moo's there?
Moos.
Moos who?
Moos you *always* ask that same
   question?

Knock, knock!
Moo's there?
Tail.
Tail who?
Tail me just *one more* "knock,
   knock," and I'm history!

Nelly: I hear you take milk baths.

Melly: That's right.

Nelly: But why?

Melly: I can't find a cow tall
enough for a shower!

MOORE
COW CROSSINGS

What do you get if you cross a cow,
a french fry, and a sofa?

A cowch potato!

What do you get if you cross a cow
and a threshing machine?

A lawn mooer!

What do you get if you cross Bossy
with a vampire?

Dracowla!

What do you get if you cross a longhorn with a knight?

Sir Loin!

What do you get if you cross a cow with a tension headache?

A bad mood!

What do you get if you cross a cow with a spaniel, a poodle, and a rooster?

A cockerpoodlemoo!

RIDICOWLOUS!

Clem: I can't decide whether to buy a bicycle or a cow for my farm.

Lem: Well, wouldn't you look silly riding a cow?

Clem: I'd look a darn sight sillier trying to milk a bicycle!

COWNT ME OUT!

Why did the farmer fence in the bull?

The farmer had too much of a steak in him to let him go!

What hair style is a calf's favorite?

The cowlick!

Why did Bossy tell the cowpoke to leave her calf alone?

She thought children should be seen and not herded!

What do you call a cow who argues with her husband?

A bullfighter!

Teacher: What is the most important use for cowhide?
Student: To hold the cow together.

BOSSY
BEST-SELLERS

Successful Milking
  by Phil D. Payle

Communicating with Cattle
  by I. Ken Mooue

Can Your Bull Be Your Pal?
  by Shirley U. Geste

Ropin' and Ranchin'
  by Larry Yett

What To Do for Bull Injuries
  by Justin K. C. Kix

Storing Your Cow Feed
  by Sy Lowe

Dealing with a Bull Charge
  by Ron Feryerlyfe

Delicious Dairy Desserts
  by Mel K. Waye

How To Organize Your Herd
  by Jess Fensum

COWNTER ATTACK!

What is a calf after it is six months old?

Seven months old!

What is the daffynition of
"derange"?

De place where de cowboys ride!

What is the daffynition of "moon"?

The past tense of "moo"!

THE TAIL END
OF THE COWTOONS

Clem: That tornado damage your
cow barn any, Lem?
Lem: Dunno. Haven't found the
durn thing yet!

BUTTER SAY GOOD-BYE!

Why did the cow yawn when she got up?

It was just an udder day!

What do you get if you cross a steer and a chicken?

Roost beef!

Why did the cow cross the road?

It was the chicken's day off!